Vocabulary
Activity Book

for ages 7-8

This CGP book is bursting with fun activities to build up children's skills and confidence.

It's ideal for extra practice to reinforce what they're learning in primary school. Enjoy!

Published by CGP

Editors:
Catherine Heygate, Nathan Mair, Hayley Shaw

With thanks to Keith Blackhall and Juliette Green for the proofreading.

With thanks to Alice Dent for the copyright research.

ISBN: 978 1 78908 991 2

Printed by Elanders Ltd, Newcastle upon Tyne.
Graphics used on the cover and throughout the book © Educlips 2022
Cover design concept by emc design ltd.

Text, design, layout and original illustrations © Coordination Group Publications Ltd. (CGP) 2022
All rights reserved.

Photocopying this book is not permitted, even if you have a CLA licence.
Extra copies are available from CGP with next day delivery • 0800 1712 712 • www.cgpbooks.co.uk

Contents

Words to do with size	2
Words to do with summer	4
Words to do with food	6
Words to do with cities	8
Words to do with emotions	10
Words that mean 'said'	12
Puzzle: Mechanical meltdown	14
Words to do with people	16
Words to do with space	18
Words to do with sound	20
Words to do with camping	22
Words to do with science	24
Words to do with time	26
Answers	28

Words to do with size

Start With This

1. Underline the word in each sentence that is to do with size.

   The lemur has a very long tail.

   Those ants are much smaller than these rhinos.

   The tiny lion cub stayed beside its mum.

Now Try These

2. Sort the words below into the correct groups.

   minute   enormous   huge   little

   Words that mean **big**:
   ....
   ....

   Words that mean **small**:
   ....
   ....

3. Circle the odd one out in each group.

   petite   dainty   giant   miniature

   great   towering   lofty   microscopic

4. Circle the word in bold that best completes each sentence.

The **lanky / squat** giraffe looked down at the other animals.

The elephant's **short / lengthy** trunk reached the highest leaves.

 That caterpillar is so **minuscule / massive** — I can barely see it!

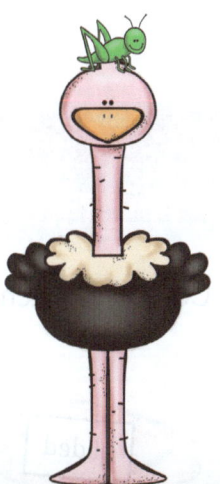

5. Write a sentence about the animals on the right.
   Use at least one word from Question 3.

   ....
   ....
   ....

An Extra Challenge

Can you find the words below in the wordsearch? Which word is the odd one out?

narrow, vast, colossal, tall, broad

b	z	i	n	a	r	r	o	w
r	f	l	v	k	h	j	x	b
o	y	u	o	c	l	d	e	g
a	e	v	a	s	t	t	h	y
d	v	z	d	p	e	a	r	j
k	u	w	d	t	r	l	c	u
s	g	t	l	b	i	l	h	a
e	w	s	a	s	e	k	h	t
n	c	o	l	o	s	s	a	l

Is talking about size a tall order? Put a tick in a box.

Words to do with summer

Start With This

1. Circle the three words that mean **hot**.

 boiling

 chilly

 mild

 breezy

 tropical

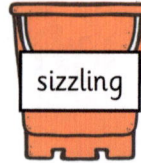 sizzling

Now Try These

2. Complete each sentence using one of the words below.

 glided

 blazing

 paradise

 refreshing

The hot summer sun was .... down.

I've just been for a swim. The water is so ....

This beach is really beautiful — it's like .... !

The surfer .... across the waves.

3. Circle two words in the text below that mean **wet**.

> Iris was soaking after falling out of her kayak. She paddled back to the shore and bundled her soggy clothes into a bag.

4. Choose a word from the box to replace each word in bold.

| strolled | peered | barbecued |

Dad **cooked** some sausages for dinner. ....

Elijah **looked** into the rock pool and saw a crab. ....

Iqra and Aisling **walked** barefoot on the sand. ....

5. There are two words that don't belong in this group. Write them on the lines.

parched   dusty   humid   waterless   muggy

....

....

An Extra Challenge

Can you come up with three sentences to describe this picture?
Use as many of the words below as you can.

scorching

splashing

lounging

disappointed

enjoyable

Are you red hot at talking about summer? Tick a box.

Words to do with food

Start With This

1. Tick the boxes next to the words that you could use to describe the cake on the right.

   sugary   large

   shallow   rich

   fancy   plain

Now Try These

2. Complete the text using the words from the boxes below.

   crumbly   fresh   spicy

   Chef Antoine is hosting a dinner party next week. He is going to prepare a ………………… salad as a starter using the vegetables from his garden. Then he will make a ………………… curry, which is his favourite dish to cook. For dessert, he is going to make a ………………… shortbread.

3. Circle the words that mean **eat**.

4. Complete each sentence using one of the words below.

That meal looks delicious. ➝ That meal looks ....

The cheese has a strong smell. ➝ The cheese has a .... smell.

The bacon is too fatty. ➝ The bacon is too ....

The dish was tasteless. ➝ The dish was ....

5. Draw lines to match each word to the right picture.

 scrumptious

revolting

An Extra Challenge

Use the clues to help you complete the crossword.

Across
3. This dish is very **faloursomev**.
4. The orange is **jiucy**.
5. The lime juice is **ganty**.

Down
1. The pastry is **fkaly**.
2. My toast is **chuncry**.

Can you cook up a delicious description? Tick a box.

Words to do with cities

Start With This

1. Circle the things that are often found in cities.

restaurant

skyscraper

cottage

art gallery

farm

Now Try These

2. Sort the words into the correct groups.

   tranquil   lively   hectic   peaceful

   Words that mean **busy**:   Words that mean **quiet**:

   ....

   ....

3. Draw lines to match the pairs of words that have opposite meanings.

clean   urban   modern   spread out

ancient   compact   polluted   rural

4. Complete each sentence using a word from the box below.

| casually | urgently | bustling | crawling | surged |

The ambulance needs to get to the hospital ....

 The bus was .... slowly into the city centre.

The cyclist pedalled through the .... streets.

 The tourist wandered .... around the museum.

The passengers .... towards the platform.

An Extra Challenge

Unscramble the words below then find them in the wordsearch.

A **srpaliwng** town takes up a lot of space.

The **subrub** is outside the city centre.

Lots of **turistos** visit the castle.

The square is really **crdwoed**.

It's a lively, **vbirnat** city.

The city is **thivrnig**.

```
a  w  s  u  b  u  r  b  j
t  e  p  a  j  c  w  v  t
h  c  r  o  w  d  e  d  o
r  r  a  s  k  v  a  t  u
i  t  w  d  l  b  s  g  r
v  y  l  f  z  n  x  b  i
i  v  i  b  r  a  n  t  s
n  u  n  g  c  m  r  y  t
g  i  g  h  x  q  f  h  s
```

Is your mind bustling with words about cities? Tick a box.

Words to do with emotions

Start With This

1. Circle the odd one out in each group.

Now Try These

2. Choose the word in bold that best completes each sentence. Use the pictures to help you.

 I was **thrilled / disappointed** when I saw an octopus.

I was **disgusted / amused** by the pufferfish.

 I was **annoyed / satisfied** that there were no piranhas.

I was **terrified / confused** by the jellyfish.

 I was **pleased / embarrassed** to see a turtle.

3. Write down a word that has the
   same meaning as each word in bold.

   The **happy** dolphin squealed in delight. ....

   The squid felt **scared** so it squirted its ink. ....

   The **tired** walrus rested on an iceberg. ....

4. Draw lines to match the pairs of words that have similar meanings.

An Extra Challenge

Use the clues to complete the words.
The letters in the blue boxes reveal a hidden sea creature.

puzzled	☐	o	n	☐	u	☐	e	d
joyful	c	h	☐	e	☐	☐	l	
afraid	☐	e	☐	r	f	☐	l	
courageous	☐	r	☐	v	☐			

The hidden animal is a:

How do you feel about describing emotions? Tick one of the boxes. ☐   ☐   ☐

Words that mean 'said'

Start With This

1. Draw a square around the words that mean **said quietly**.
   Draw a circle around the words that mean **said loudly**.

 yelled
 hissed
 muttered
 murmured
 bellowed
 roared

Now Try These

2. Circle the word in bold that best completes each sentence.

 Tamara **called / muttered** to Adam from the other side of the playground.

 "It's dinner time," Thea **whispered / announced** loudly to the room full of gossiping guests.

Deji didn't hear what Evie said because she was **shouting / mumbling**.

 "It's a bit scary all the way up here," Reuben **stammered / ordered** from the treetops.

3. Write a sentence of your own using one of the words from Question 1.

   ....

   ....

4. Underline the word in each sentence that means **said**. Draw a line to the right balloon to show whether it means **said happily** or **said sadly**.

"Hooray!" Clive cheered when his team won.

Adaku groaned that the hill was too steep.

"I don't want to go," Frankie sighed.

Freddie sobbed that his leg hurt.

"I love yellow balloons," Saffiya chuckled.

"The view is fantastic," beamed Alexis.

5. Write down a word that could replace **said** in each sentence. Use a different word each time.

"I hate eating sprouts!" **said** Jemima.   ....

Mr Chopra **said** he would come to the party.   ....

"Buster come back!" **said** Piotr.   ....

An Extra Challenge

How many different words for **said** can you spot in this passage?

"I'm going to the park," declared Camilla.

"I want to come with you!" her neighbour Kai demanded.

"Of course!" Camilla exclaimed.

While they were playing, Camilla spotted a llama on the seesaw.

"Look!" she cried.

"How unusual!" Kai gasped.

How happy are you with words for said? Give a box a tick.

Words to do with people

Start With This

1. Match each word to the right picture.

 friendly

hostile

Now Try These

2. Use the words in the boxes to fill in the gaps in the text.

   hardworking   talented   caring

   Sally is a .... woman — she is good at lots of things.
   She likes looking after other people and .... for them.
   That's why she became a paramedic. It's not an easy job, but Sally is very
   .... and always tries her best.

3. Circle the odd one out in each group.

    brave    adventurous    cheerful

    shy    gloomy    jolly

4. Circle the two words that mean **thoughtful**.

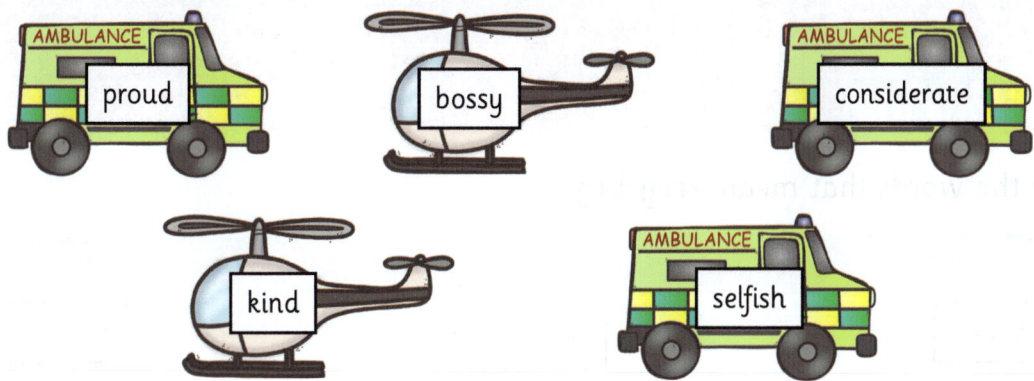

5. Write a sentence of your own using two of the words from Question 4.

   ....

   ....

6. Circle the word in bold that best completes each sentence.

   My next door neighbour always says "Good morning!" to me — he is very **polite / irritable**.

   He was very **dishonest / frank** and told me exactly what he was thinking.

An Extra Challenge

Write two sentences about each of the people in this scene.

Try to use one word from these pages in each sentence.

Have you got to know the words on these pages? Tick a box.

17

Words to do with space

Start With This

1. Circle the words that mean **very big**.

 slender
 enormous
 measly

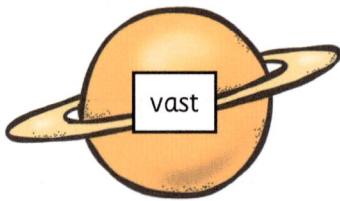 vast
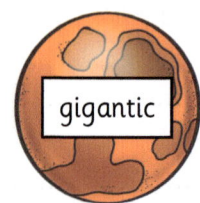 gigantic
 round

Now Try These

2. Using a dictionary to help you, match each word to its definition.

galaxy — a large ball of hot gas in space

orbit — a group of stars and planets

star — glowing

luminous — travel around a planet, moon or star

3. Write a sentence of your own using two words from Question 2.

....

....

4. For each word, write another word that means the same thing.

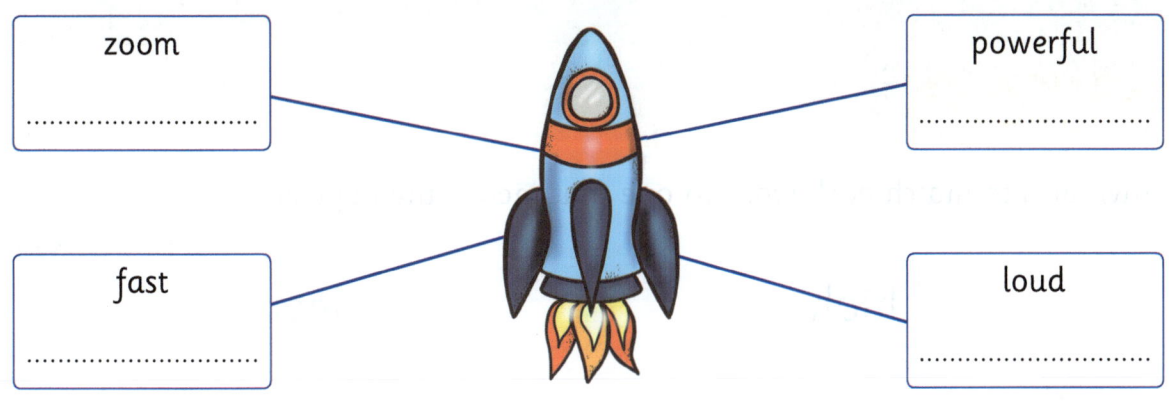

zoom ....

powerful ....

fast ....

loud ....

5. Circle the word in bold that best completes each sentence.

We depend on **satellites / sunset** for our mobile phones to work.

What **pose / position** is the spacecraft in?

Space rockets can experience **extreme / long** temperatures during take-off and landing.

An Extra Challenge

Unscramble the words in bold and then find them in the wordsearch.

an **asuortnat** travels to space

lnadnig on a planet requires lots of preparation

Earth is a **lpneta**

```
a s t r o n a u t
b k a z w s x d e
p b g n e l c r l
l l f v t a g h e
a p m o o n s j s
n o u j g d l m c
e i j a e i b n o
t a l i e n s c p
y u h g f g d x e
```

slaien are from outer space

Mars has two **sonom**

use a **teelcsoep** to see a long way

Have you found space for these words in your head? Tick a box.

Words to do with sound

Start With This

1. Draw lines to match each word to one that means the opposite.

high   clear

noisy   low

muffled   quiet

Now Try These

2. Circle the odd one out.

     thunk   twitch   howl   honk

3. Choose a word from below to complete each sentence. Use each word once.

Can you hear them .... the drums?

 He's a terrible singer — it's like listening to a bird .... !

The cymbals made a loud .... as Salima knocked them over.

 Timmy's voice .... around the cave.

4. Write down a word to replace the word in bold in each sentence.

Ellie likes to play her trumpet **loudly** at 5 am.

....

Sometimes I listen to **gentle** music to help me sleep.

....

When Si started playing the saxophone, he could barely make a **squeak**.

....

When the orchestra finished, there was a **deafening** round of applause.

....

An Extra Challenge

Use these clues to complete the crossword.

Across

1. If you drop something, it makes a **lactret**.
4. Trumpets go **otto**.
5. Shhh — **scileen** please.

Down

2. **Tuhd** went the drums.
3. The baby's toy **tratles**.

Does it sound like you know these words? Tick a box.

21

Words to do with camping

Start With This

1. Circle three words that mean **a long way away**.

 remote
 nearby
 huge
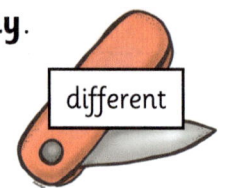 different
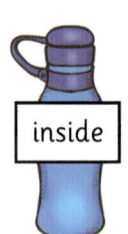 inside
 far-off
 distant

Now Try These

2. Circle the word that means:

   in the countryside —  rural    field    green

   no-one lives there —  city    housing    deserted

   doesn't let water in —  sopping    waterproof    soft

3. Circle the word in bold that best completes each sentence.

   Our tent is made from light **material / boulders** so it is easy to carry.

   Inside, it is very **spacious / separate**.

4. Read this postcard. Replace each word in bold with a different word that means the same thing.

Dear Nick,

We're having a **fantastic** .... time on our camping trip. Although it is **freezing** .... at night and sometimes **foggy** .... in the mornings, the area is very **scenic** .... Hopefully you can join us next time!

Nick McCard

37 North Street

Middleton

South Castleshire

MD1 7HR

5. Write down a word that has the opposite meaning to each word in bold.

We toasted **delicious** marshmallows.

It was very **safe**. ....

An Extra Challenge

Which of the words below could you use to describe this scene?

crowded   wild   peaceful

busy   ugly   mountainous

Can you use each of the words you've chosen in a sentence?

Are you feeling wild about these words? Give yourself a tick.

Words to do with science

Start With This

1. Oops! Someone has removed all the labels from the science equipment. Draw lines to show which label goes on each object.

magnet

microscope

safety goggles

thermometer

Now Try These

2. Match each word to one that means the opposite.

natural   see-through

solid   repel

opaque   artificial

attract   liquid

3. Use words from Question 2 to fill in the gaps in these science facts.

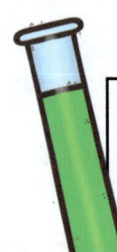

The Sun is a .... source of light.

When you freeze water, it becomes a ....

4. Label the picture using the words in the box.

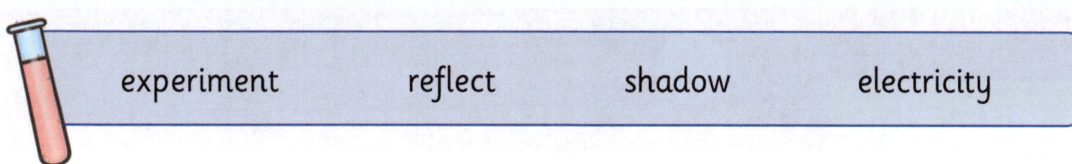

experiment   reflect   shadow   electricity

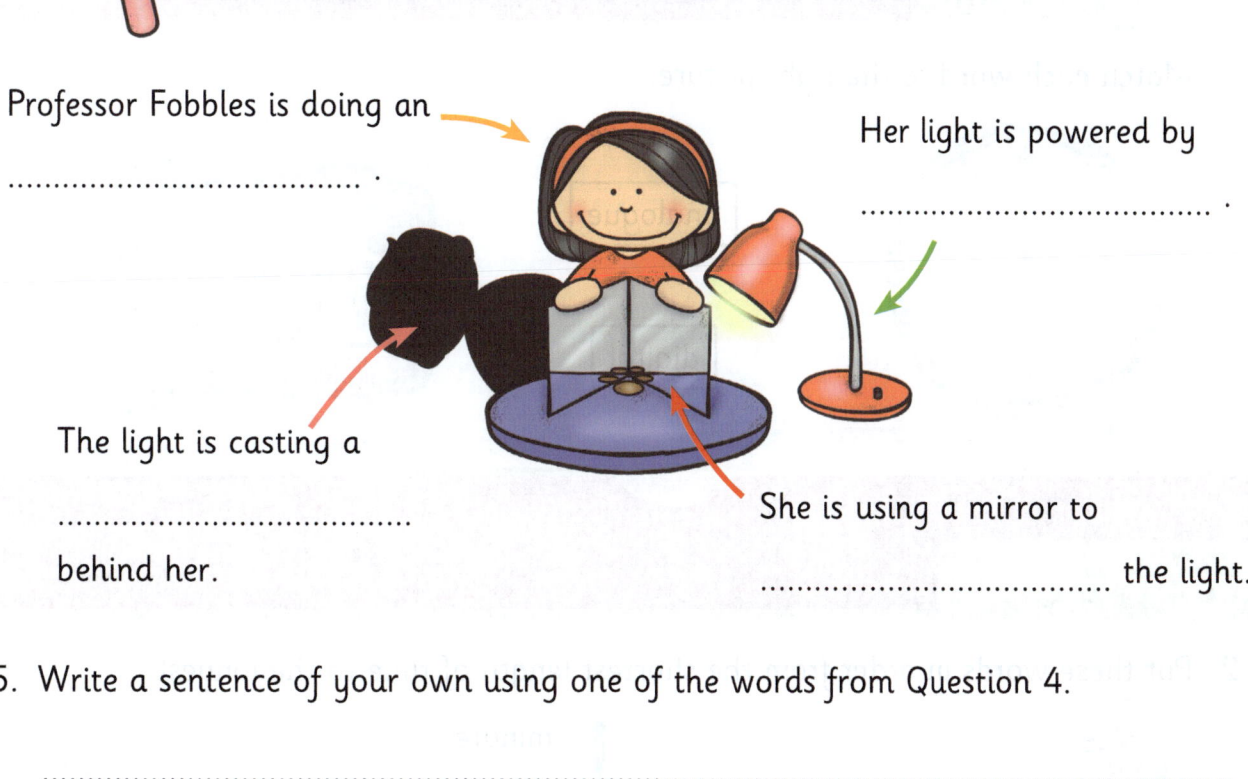

Professor Fobbles is doing an

....

The light is casting a

....

behind her.

Her light is powered by

....

She is using a mirror to

.... the light.

5. Write a sentence of your own using one of the words from Question 4.

....

....

An Extra Challenge

Crack the code and work out these top-secret science words.

a	b	c	d	e	f	g	h	i	j	k	l	m	n	o	p	q	r	s	t	u	v	w	x	y	z
1	2	3	4	5	6	7	8	9	0	-	=	[	]	;	~	#	,	/	?	!	^	*	&	(	+

;2/5,^5

6;,35/

6,93?9;]

6=1[5

Do you know what they mean? Look up any you aren't sure about in a dictionary.

Have you discovered all these words? Tick a box.

Words to do with time

Start With This

1. Match each word to the right picture.

analogue

digital

Now Try These

2. Put these words in order from the shortest length of time to the longest.

minute

month

year

....

....

decade

....

day

....

century

3. Circle the word that means **midday**.

mid-afternoon

sunset

evening

noon

4. Choose a word from the box that means the same thing as each word in bold.

delayed   fleeting   era

There was a **brief** rain shower.

The Victorian **period** lasted for 63 years.

The train was **late**.

....

5. Circle the option in bold that best completes each sentence.

My **calendar / clock** shows that I'm going to a party later today.

Christmas is **a monthly / an annual** event.

The Romans lived in **ancient / recent** times.

6. Write a sentence of your own using one of the words from Question 4.

....

....

An Extra Challenge

All the clocks at the castle have stopped working. Unscramble these words to help the knights find the time.

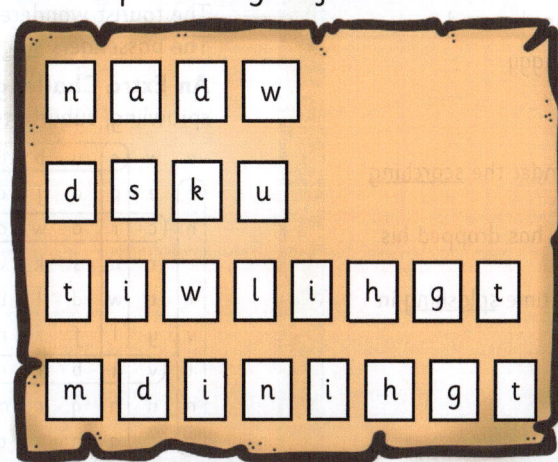

n a d w

d s k u

t i w l i h g t

m d i n i h g t

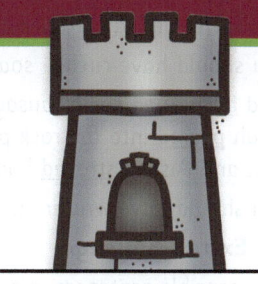

Which two words have similar meanings?

Have you spent enough time on these words? Tick a box.

27

Answers

Pages 2-3 — Words to do with size

1. The lemur has a very <u>long</u> tail.
   Those ants are much <u>smaller</u> than these rhinos.
   The <u>tiny</u> lion cub stayed beside its mum.
2. Words that mean **big**: enormous, huge
   Words that mean **small**: minute, little
3. You should have circled: giant, microscopic
4. The <u>lanky</u> giraffe looked down at the other animals.
   The elephant's <u>lengthy</u> trunk reached the highest leaves.
   That caterpillar is so <u>minuscule</u> — I can barely see it!
5. Any sensible sentence, e.g.
   The <u>miniature</u> grasshopper is sitting on the <u>towering</u> ostrich.

An Extra Challenge

b	z	i	n	a	r	r	o	w
r	f	l	v	k	h	j	x	b
o	y	u	o	c	l	d	e	g
a	e	v	a	s	t	t	h	y
d	v	z	d	p	e	a	r	j
k	u	w	d	t	r	l	c	u
s	g	t	l	b	i	l	h	a
e	w	s	a	s	e	k	h	t
n	c	o	l	o	s	s	a	l

'narrow' is the odd one out.

Pages 4-5 — Words to do with summer

1. You should have circled: boiling, tropical, sizzling
2. The hot summer sun was <u>blazing</u> down.
   I've just been for a swim. The water is so <u>refreshing</u>.
   This beach is really beautiful — it's like <u>paradise</u>!
   The surfer <u>glided</u> across the waves.
3. You should have circled: soaking, soggy
4. Dad <u>barbecued</u> some sausages for dinner.
   Elijah <u>peered</u> into the rock pool and saw a crab.
   Iqra and Aisling <u>strolled</u> barefoot on the sand.
5. You should have written: humid, muggy

An Extra Challenge

Any sensible sentences, e.g.
The girl is <u>lounging</u> on the beach under the <u>scorching</u> sun.
The boy is <u>disappointed</u> because he has dropped his ice cream.
The dolphin is having an <u>enjoyable</u> time <u>splashing</u> in the sea.

Pages 6-7 — Words to do with food

1. You should have ticked: sugary, large, rich, fancy
2. Chef Antoine is hosting a dinner party next week. He is going to prepare a <u>fresh</u> salad as a starter using the vegetables from his garden. Then he will make a <u>spicy</u> curry, which is his favourite dish to cook. For dessert, he is going to make a <u>crumbly</u> shortbread.
3. You should have circled: savour, nibble, devour
4. That meal looks <u>appetising</u>.
   The cheese has a <u>pungent</u> smell.
   The bacon is too <u>greasy</u>.
   The dish was <u>bland</u>.
5. scrumptious / revolting

An Extra Challenge

Across
3. flavoursome
4. juicy
5. tangy

Down
1. flaky
2. crunchy

Pages 8-9 — Words to do with cities

1. You should have circled: restaurant, skyscraper, art gallery
2. Words that mean **busy**: lively, hectic
   Words that mean **quiet**: tranquil, peaceful
3. clean — polluted
   urban — rural
   modern — ancient
   spread out — compact
4. The ambulance needs to get to the hospital <u>urgently</u>.
   The bus was <u>crawling</u> slowly into the city centre.
   The cyclist pedalled through the <u>bustling</u> streets.
   The tourist wandered <u>casually</u> around the museum.
   The passengers <u>surged</u> towards the platform.

An Extra Challenge

sprawling, suburb, tourists, crowded, vibrant, thriving

a	w	s	u	b	u	r	b	j
t	e	p	a	j	c	w	v	t
h	c	r	o	w	d	e	d	o
r	r	a	s	k	v	a	t	u
i	t	w	d	l	b	s	g	r
v	y	l	f	z	n	x	b	i
i	v	i	b	r	a	n	t	s
n	u	n	g	c	m	r	y	t
g	i	g	h	x	q	f	h	s

Answers

Pages 10-11 — Words to do with emotions

1. You should have circled: tense, glad
2. I was <u>thrilled</u> when I saw an octopus.
   I was <u>amused</u> by the pufferfish.
   I was <u>annoyed</u> that there were no piranhas.
   I was <u>terrified</u> by the jellyfish.
   I was <u>pleased</u> to see a turtle.
3. Any sensible words with similar meanings, e.g. delighted, terrified, exhausted
4. confident — positive
   nervous — anxious
   envious — jealous

   An Extra Challenge
   confused, cheerful, fearful, brave
   The hidden animal is a: crab

Pages 12-13 — Words that mean 'said'

1. Words that mean **said quietly**: hissed, muttered, murmured
   Words that mean **said loudly**: yelled, bellowed, roared
2. Tamara <u>called</u> to Adam from the other side of the playground.
   "It's dinner time," Thea <u>announced</u> loudly to the room full of gossiping guests.
   Deji didn't hear what Evie said because she was <u>mumbling</u>.
   "It's a bit scary all the way up here," Reuben <u>stammered</u> from the treetops.
3. Any sensible sentence, e.g.
   Miss Herbert <u>bellowed</u> at the class to come inside.
4. **said happily**:
   "Hooray!" Clive <u>cheered</u> when his team won.
   "I love yellow balloons," Saffiya <u>chuckled</u>.
   "The view is fantastic," <u>beamed</u> Alexis.
   said sadly:
   Adaku <u>groaned</u> that the hill was too steep.
   "I don't want to go," Frankie <u>sighed</u>.
   Freddie <u>sobbed</u> that his leg hurt.
5. Any sensible words that could replace said, e.g. moaned, promised, squealed

   An Extra Challenge
   declared, demanded, exclaimed, cried, gasped

Pages 14-15 — Mechanical meltdown

shiny: gleaming, metallic, polished, glossy
sounds: clunk, jangle, whirr, whistle
machine: engine, appliance, gadget, device
The odd word out is: inventor

Pages 16-17 — Words to do with people

1.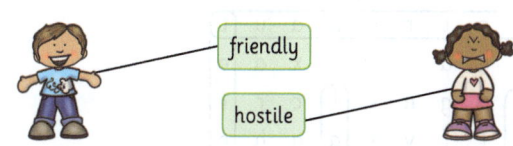

2. Sally is a <u>talented</u> woman — she is good at lots of things. She likes looking after other people and <u>caring</u> for them. That's why she became a paramedic. It's not an easy job, but Sally is very <u>hardworking</u> and always tries her best.
3. You should have circled: shy, gloomy
4. You should have circled: considerate, kind
5. Any sensible sentence, e.g.
   Dhruv is <u>kind</u> and always lets me play with his toys, but Kia is very <u>selfish</u> — she doesn't like to share.
6. My next door neighbour always says "Good morning!" to me — he is very <u>polite</u>.
   He was very <u>frank</u> and told me exactly what he was thinking.

   An Extra Challenge
   Any sensible sentences, e.g.
   The police officer has to be <u>polite</u> when passers-by ask her what's happening.
   The fireman was very <u>brave</u> when he climbed the tree.

Pages 18-19 — Words to do with space

1. You should have circled: enormous, vast, gigantic
2. galaxy — a group of stars and planets
   orbit — travel around a planet, moon or star
   star — a large ball of hot gas in space
   luminous — glowing
3. Any sensible sentence, e.g.
   The Sun is a <u>star</u> in our <u>galaxy</u>.
4. Any sensible words, e.g.
   zoom — whoosh
   powerful — mighty
   fast — rapid
   loud — roaring
5. We depend on <u>satellites</u> for our mobile phones to work.
   What <u>position</u> is the spacecraft in?
   Space rockets can experience <u>extreme</u> temperatures during take-off and landing.

Answers

An Extra Challenge

astronaut, landing, planet, aliens, moons, telescope

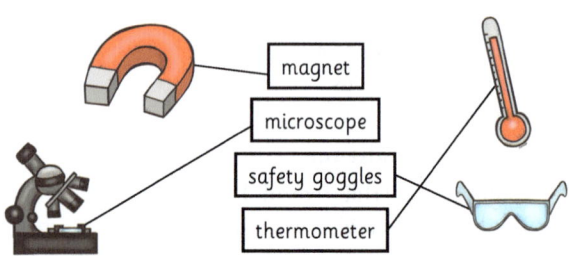

Pages 20-21 — Words to do with sound

1. high — low
   noisy — quiet
   muffled — clear

2. You should have circled: twitch

3. Can you hear them <u>beating</u> the drums?
   He's a terrible singer — it's like listening to a bird <u>screech</u>!
   The cymbals made a loud <u>crash</u> as Salima knocked them over.
   Timmy's voice <u>echoed</u> around the cave.

4. Any sensible words with similar meanings, e.g.
   noisily, calm, peep, thunderous

   An Extra Challenge

   Across   Down
   1. clatter   2. thud
   4. toot   3. rattles
   5. silence

Pages 22-23 — Words to do with camping

1. You should have circled: remote, far-off, distant

2. in the countryside — rural
   no-one lives there — deserted
   doesn't let water in — waterproof

3. Our tent is made from light <u>material</u> so it is easy to carry.
   Inside, it is very <u>spacious</u>.

4. Any sensible answers, e.g.
   We're having a <u>wonderful</u> time on our camping trip. Although it is <u>icy</u> at night and sometimes <u>misty</u> in the mornings, the area is very <u>beautiful</u>.

5. Any sensible words, e.g. disgusting, dangerous

An Extra Challenge

wild, peaceful, mountainous
Any sensible sentences, e.g.
The area is very <u>wild</u>.
We like to visit <u>peaceful</u> places on holiday.
Scotland is very <u>mountainous</u>.

Pages 24-25 — Words to do with science

1. magnet, microscope, safety goggles, thermometer

2. natural — artificial
   solid — liquid
   opaque — see-through
   attract — repel

3. The Sun is a <u>natural</u> source of light.
   When you freeze water, it becomes a <u>solid</u>.

4. Professor Fobbles is doing an <u>experiment</u>.
   Her light is powered by <u>electricity</u>.
   The light is casting a <u>shadow</u> behind her.
   She is using a mirror to <u>reflect</u> the light.

5. Any sensible sentence, e.g.
   At school today, we carried out an <u>experiment</u> on a plant.

An Extra Challenge

observe, forces, friction, flame

Pages 26-27 — Words to do with time

1. analogue, digital

2. day, month, year, decade

3. You should have circled: noon

4. fleeting, era, delayed

5. My <u>calendar</u> shows that I'm going to a party later today.
   Christmas is <u>an annual</u> event.
   The Romans lived in <u>ancient</u> times.

6. Any sensible sentence, e.g.
   The concert was <u>delayed</u> because Gary lost his tuba.

An Extra Challenge

dawn, dusk, twilight, midnight
Twilight and dusk have similar meanings.